dear terror, dear splendor

WISCONSIN POETRY SERIES

Edited by Ronald Wallace

dear terror, dear splendor

melissa crowe

THE UNIVERSITY OF WISCONSIN PRESS

Publication of this volume has been made possible, in part, through support from the Brittingham Trust.

The University of Wisconsin Press
1930 Monroe Street, 3rd Floor
Madison, Wisconsin 53711-2059
uwpress.wisc.edu

Gray's Inn House, 127 Clerkenwell Road
London EC1R 5DB, United Kingdom
eurospanbookstore.com

Printed in the United States of America

This book may be available in a digital edition.

Library of Congress Cataloging-in-Publication Data

Names: Crowe, Melissa, author.
Title: Dear terror, dear splendor / Melissa Crowe.
Other titles: Wisconsin poetry series.
Description: Madison, Wisconsin : The University of Wisconsin Press,
          [2019] | Series: Wisconsin poetry series
Identifiers: LCCN 2018040964 | ISBN 9780299321444 (pbk.; alk. paper)
Subjects: | LCGFT: Poetry.
Classification: LCC PS3603.R689 D43 2019 | DDC 811/.6—dc23
LC record available at https://lccn.loc.gov/2018040964

CONTENTS

III.

IV.

V.

dear
terror,
dear
splendor

This River

There are uncles at the bottom
of this river, bird bones, boats, a whole
blue-lipped summer; we drink
the water and are filled with uncles
and birds, filled with fish eyes,
tadpoles, our throats velvet
as the burst heads of cattail,
the drunkenness of uncles wobbling
from their boats, and the time
we kissed a boy in the low mud
beneath the cattail, leaving the shape
of our bodies and the ghosts
of our sighs; we drink mud and sighs
and are filled with emptiness, and still
we drink our uncles like stones and sink
to the bottom of memory where
we look up through the water and see
the dizzy light of stars as dead
as uncles and a blur of birds
that seem unsinkable in flight.

I.

To refuse to be born is one thing—
but once you are here,
you'd do well to stop crying
and suck the good milk in.

rita dove

French Food

Presque Isle, Maine, 1980

We ate *creton*—paste of pig's head
and onion. We ate deer steak fried

in grease and blood, government cheese
in waxy orange blocks. Some meals

come almost free—if you'll forage,
if you'll hunt—and we did,

the purple meat of rabbits
graying in our big tin pot.

We ate trout after trout, their silver bellies
battered, white flesh threaded

with tiny bones and sometimes worms.
We ate fiddleheads—baby ferns,

tight curls loosening in brackish
water, melted butter. Potatoes

hauled up daily from the cellar dark
never lost their dirt scent, their dirt

taste, no matter how scrubbed
and peeled and charred.

While we ate, we breathed kerosene—
skunk and blood and lilac—mixed

with my grandfather's sweat, rising
from his work clothes.

It blackened his hands and seasoned
our stews, our slices of spongy

white bread sopping kerosene
off the air, off our plates. We swallowed

all of this and knew just where
we were and who.

The Uncles

steal for you kittens and bicycles, build garbage fires
in the yard, the sour heat a kind of magic, and cupping hands
to mouths they make harmonica music, but when they spread
their fingers: air—
                    the uncles are everywhere—
                                              thumbing
fish guts in the sink, motoring the street on painted hogs,
and when they pull you up, helmetless in your sundress,
your legs burn, till eyes closed, clutching, there's nothing
but sweat and uncle and speed—
                              the uncles eat onions
like apples, need hot dogs and pain meds, their pelvises
in pieces from the car wreck, they ask you to barefoot
their bare backs, give you silver dollars for the service,
and with their soft red afros and muscled chests
and good voices for country, they sing Mammas
Don't Let Your Babies Grow Up, their hooks dangling
the creek—
          they cook trout on a grill of concrete blocks
lifted from construction sites, the scent of smoke
and fat and joy—
                the uncles live in your house or in trailers
or with girlfriends or ex-girlfriends, women with leather vests
and ass-length, white-blond hair—
                                  the uncles work at the fair,
reek of kerosene and fried dough, sneak you in
through a fence hole, tin snips and arm scrapes, and summers
you slip into the public pool after hours, silence of night
and slap of water and laughter of uncles—
                                        and when the cops come,
as they do, you cry, the uncles in cuffs, their forearms

like fish bellies knife-slit in a bar fight or their heels crushed,
chased over cliff edge or roof edge by the husband
of some white-blond woman who maybe cries with you
in the kitchen, one uncle dragged away—

                          but *don't worry*,
you say, there are other uncles where that uncle came from,
you're sure one split uncle can pour forth more, like scarves
from a sleeve—you have to believe in a stream of particolored
uncles, endless as a sky tattooed with prison-blue stars.

Kissing Lessons

My mother taught me the dry, tight-lipped kind,
on the cheek before the bus, at bedtime, tested
my forehead for fever with her chapsticked lips.

Men and women did it on TV, long, open as a yawn,
with tongues. I called it *movie-star kissing*, asked Gram
how they breathed, already suspected being grown

meant some low tingle mixed with sacrifice,
that there are people who will suffocate
for love. My father gone, a tall man took my mother

to Niagara Falls. Scraggly bearded and slow limbed,
he came in a taxi to take her to the airport. For three days
I played Crazy Eights and watched *Fantasy Island*

with Big Diane whose rooms connected to ours
through a shared toilet. Leaned against her softness,
I tracked with tired eyes Mr. Roarke and Tattoo,

girls in short wrap dresses and men with tails
and hooves, sex and mist and voodoo. Later that night
I pretended to sleep and she shifted me to a pillow,

padded through the bathroom. The gritty, metal give
of her deadbolt said Little Andrew was there, five feet tall
and barely a hundred pounds, and Big Diane told Gram

he did it like a butterfly, long lashes fluttering her lips,
her lobes, her neck. When the man returned my mother
after the long weekend, they lingered on the steps.

The screen door grayed and distanced
Mama's auburn hair, her thin arms, and they kissed
like in the movies, but my mother kept one hand

between their bodies like you'd press to keep
a door closed. That night in bed I made a fist
of my fingers, forced my tongue into its mouth.

Cirque du Crève-Cœur

Sixth-grade best friend—
your wallpaper with its perfect
white trellis, its smooth

seams (chosen perhaps
and glued when you
nestled zygotic in their

dreams) meant your parents
wanted you. The shag carpet
smelled like shampoo,

a piano in the living room.
There was nothing special
about you, nothing I can

explain, only that I loved you
with frightening passion
when we pretended

to be tigers, pretended
to be girls on the high wire,
tails of satin and bare legs,

when we sold tickets
and your mother ate popcorn
and watched us roar and flail

and afterward I lay beside you
on your bed, the canopy blue
as a true vista, where I proposed

that we should grow to be
women and live together
in California. The sides of our

hands touched, my left pinky
and your right pinky pressed
between us, and you

didn't swear (the sharp air,
my sudden fall). You didn't
answer at all.

Mourning Portrait for Uncle Steve

Because of you I never believed when anybody
called anybody a bad man for some bad thing
he'd done. I knew you—gentle, funny,
generous—on furlough from Thomaston

where you'd serve ten years
for shooting a man without meaning
to kill him. And my aunt, leaning out of a decade
of psychosis and psoriasis, married you in jail.

Monthly she drove the hundred miles
in her seventies sedan, and along for the ride
I sprawled the backseat with my cousins,
watching pavement pour past

through a rusted hole in the floor, its edges
ragged, its allure magnetic to my eyes, already
tuned to escape. At the prison, I waited in the car,
so I'm only imagining a room like a cafeteria,

tables that smelled of sour rags, flanked
by vending machines stocked with Baby Ruth
and Tab, cousins smudging the glass
with their empty hands while Aunt Jolene

spent her touch-free half hour in your company.
But I remember the days after your early release,
the barbeque at your mother's house, where we
celebrated your freedom with charred chicken legs

and homemade pickles and ear after ear of corn,
so sweet and bright. At dusk you took us kids
into an empty field and lit sparklers
with your Bic. You handed off each burning,

spitting stick like a borrowed cigarette
for us to hold fearfully or wave fast, figure eights
of light against the blackening sky. And even later,
while you played harmonica on the porch

and the cousins danced in tall grass
and a garbage fire smoked and the blue light
outside the screen door devoured mosquitoes
with a staccato of electric snaps, I found

a stack of family albums in the cupboard
under the TV in your mother's living room
and turned their pages till horror overcame
curiosity: snapshot after snapshot of dead children,

their tiny faces pinched and powdered,
limbs arranged in christening gowns
against the padded satin of their coffins.
I'd see those faces in dreams for years

and yours, too. Not long freed,
you got a job on a harvester and one dawn
sat at a crossroads in the pickup
of the guy you'd bummed a ride from.

Maybe he was shaking off sleep
or hung over or just stupid. In any case
he inched into the intersection of those two
farm roads seconds before a Mack truck

crushed everything we thought would happen
when you got out. I don't believe you get
what you deserve or that good things
come to those who wait, and I don't

believe either that every picture's worth
a thousand words. Some give rise mainly
to silence, a set of little losses, their mouths
shut tight against goodbye.

Old Man and Nurse

My grandfather is dying slowly and with much glee
always pleased to see me though he can't tell
who I am. He writes the weather on scraps of paper
he tucks into his jeans and when I arrive
he unfolds what the week will bring—
on Monday, clear skies, on Tuesday, *wrinkles*
and headstorms, more of same till week's end:
beware. He watches TV six hours one day
waiting to see a commercial in which a girl he likes
drinks juice. Her pigtails coiled, her fat cheeks sweet,
she is the me he remembers but doesn't know
I am. *There's my girl*, he says when she appears.
There she is, I say as I pull the plug. He will think
the set is broken and when I return to fit the prongs
into their holes, oh what he will make of me, so clever,
fixer of TVs, opener of jelly packets he tries to spread whole
on toast, bringer of bottles of Pepsi and pain pills, not his girl
but someone equally nice, someone whose name
escapes him now as I rub salve on his shingles,
as I fluff the pillow where he will lay his head, puff
of white hair, thick and greased. Not his girl, I kiss
his sunken face and know whoever we may be
he has loved us both, that girl and me.

Instead of Prayer

I press your frozen
face between my palms,

your steel-drum chest
unbreathing. You still

smell like you: clean sweat,
hair oil, ghost of the gasoline

you pumped for forty years.
You'll be buried in work

clothes because you don't
have others and because

your son wants God
to know you at the gate.

Instead of prayer, I press
my face to yours, sandpaper

over stone. I kiss this death
that wears my grandfather's

body, his worn blue shirt,
dry scent. I touch all this

because it's what
you left me

and because even this
inheritance will lie,

tomorrow, well beyond
mouths and hands.

Minimalist's Manifesto

I want to believe I'd have thrived
on wolf milk, slept sound

in the crook of a paw. Instead,
in a bed under cracked glass,

I wore my winter coat.
Hat and mittens and scarf.

Some kind of slivering
down instead of growth,

some kind of nearing
needlessness—no

electricity, no
dial tone, no

toilet paper
or bread.

At seventeen I stayed
in the empty house

without money
or mother—father,

sister, brother
gone off to await

her carving out,
her uncancering.

I swore I could live
on nothing. Now

like the pack that taught me
their make-do ways, I imagine

I could: lean animal stalking
heartbeats in the wood,

just the sound of blood
enough. I don't eat

rabbits. I eat noise
and air and light.

Or I eat the silent,
moonless night.

Whatever there is, I'm
alright. Whatever there

isn't. Alone I carve
each craving to its bone.

A Laying On of Hands

The moon rose ringed one night
that winter, its areola of soft light
like an omen. Sister and brother,
babies, slept, and my mother too sick

to give a damn about the moon
lay on the couch, her tail of rubber
tubed into a plastic sack of urine
on the floor. Outside I stood

with the man who had become
my father, the driveway an ice slick
pocked with salt. He said he wondered
if such a moon was beautiful.

Shuddering with love
and shame, I'd held a boy
inside myself the night before
and thought the same—

was it sweet or terrible,
that first sex, while downstairs
my mother scratched her burns
and called for me to fill her cup

with ice. Like some saint shedding
fingers or breasts, she grew large
as she diminished, and in the ring
around the moon I saw our lives,

each of us a separate shard
refracting her disease.
My dad and I stared hard
at the sky, and from the corner

of my eye I saw his head, bare
and fogged with breath, somehow
prayerful though upturned
instead of bowed. I wonder now

if we wished the same,
my mother well but also the right
for us to feel good, even if
she never would again.

II.

I'm a small stone, loose in the shale.
Love is my wound.

theodore roethke

Grounded

Earth's the right place for love:
I don't know where it's likely to go better.
ROBERT FROST

I was eleven years old when I decided to stay on this planet—
girl meets astronaut, plans moonwalk, spacewalk, untethered
swoon, hieroglyphs of smoke write disaster

against the Cape Canaveral sky. That year my mother
miscarried twice, and I knew a kid who died at sleep-away camp—
bee-stung reading comics in her bunk, my cousin killed

coming home from fishing—summer dusk,
some drunk in the wrong lane. The U.S. bombed Libya
and I watched *Alex: The Life of a Child* till the tape snapped,

all that blood in the sink and the moment she thinks
she sees God. Born to a teen barmaid and a married
alcoholic, I saw Michael Reagan tell Donahue

illegitimate children can't be saved, ransacked
my Bible for that lie, then stopped going to church,
called myself an atheist, an atheist, stubborn litany

that made my best friend cry. *You'll never go to heaven,*
she sobbed at the slumber party. *None of us are going*
anywhere, I told her. Wouldn't allow myself

the seventy-three seconds that crew believed they'd break out.
Never mind there are footprints in the lunar dust. Never mind
there are those who know how this place looks—*pale blue*

25

dot—from up there. Down here, my stepfather wakes
soaked in my mother's blood again, and I bite every prayer
that sneaks into my mouth till I taste metal. Down here,

sixteen, I spot you in Spanish class and am filled with heat
and light, the way your lips move—*eres tu, eres tu*—
your kind eyes the color of your faded jeans, and I know

what this means: I'll have to lift off in ill-starred
conditions every day. I'll have to speed toward the breach,
burning with belief, second after second after second.

Epithalamium with Acrobats

Ah, love, let us be clowns to one another
our mouths drawn down, yes, but
every frown and tear merely
grease paint. Let's see how many
of us can fit into a car, a suitcase,
a flaming hoop until your orange
poof burns up and when you cry out
the crowd howls—oh, love, the hilarity
of a clown on fire, the polka-dot
tie, and I make a show of hopping
on my false feet in my giant pants,
waving my arms and squeezing
the bulb on my trick corsage, all this
mock triage, but you never could
die, nobody laughs at a dead clown,
you just fall down and pop up
like a weeble. Love, what do you say,
let's be lions together, big cats
on tiny stools, swatting the man
with the bull whip so he sweats lead,
until he puts his head in our toothy
mouths, a daily feat, and we are
bored and maybe
hungry, and nobody can tell quite
what we'll do for meat. Let's be
girls on the high wire, spangled
and earnest, hurtling to clasp
hands, the silence of held breath
in the stands. Let's lie in bed afterward
in our red tent eating peanuts
and unlacing our costumes, our kisses

salty exhalations, love, let us be
love to one another, ridiculous,
ferocious, brave.

Southbound Epithalamium

You ask me to accept this winterlessness,
and I do. I bare shy knees and drink sweet tea
in January, July, abide your fist-fat magnolia petals

rotting the lawn, your blistering brick walks
where sleepy lizards pink, and in the cracks
perhaps the widow spider, brown recluse.

I won't miss the terror of driving back roads,
black ice and deer eyes till the house appears,
solid and with its pocket of secret heat.

Yes, I relinquish the danger of December
and its deliciousness, short precious days,
mornings spent sitting by the eastern-facing

window, eyes trained on the light. It's alright.
But know where I go I carry this cheek-chapped
northern girl. Wool-wrapped, she trudges

her mother's boot prints from front door
to bus stop in predawn's impossible blue.
Or now, unbundled, follows you.

Love Song to a Cashier

Whither thou goest, husband, I imagine you
slipping on ice or treated cruelly
by supervisors who have never smelled
your ears and who don't know
the down of your belly

so I go behind you to the market secretly
little department of security
so I go between you
and the shooter, the microbe, the bitch
in my mind, *ohming* my way

into your day, to see that you are
handled kingly, whispered
sweetly, that the man who buys
broccoli for his dogs
gentles his money into your palm.

Elegy with F Words

Fuck the unalterable fact of my eventual unbeing.
Fuck my right ear, out of which I don't hear so well anymore.
Fuck Coca-Cola, delicious eroder of teeth and moods.
Fuck my brother, addicted to painkillers, who won't stop stealing all our
  father's shit (and fuck the memory of that brother, two years old,
  sitting in my lap, singing "Why Don't We Do It in the Road").
Fuck the light for falling so briefly upon our winter days, so that my
  husband, sun-hungry, scowls and swears and curses the
  government and the corporations and jerks who ride his ass all
  the way to the grocery store.
Fuck his long purple fingers and his ears that smell like sugar and soap
  (and fuck fucking, while we're at it).
Fuck overloads and outcomes and book orders and syllabi (and that
  student's brilliant thesis on feminist robots).
Fuck the fucking cosmos for being infinite, and fuck you, awesome
  infinity, for keeping me up nights and eluding my
  comprehension.
Fuck Carl Sagan for talking like that and for making me love him in
  spite of it.
Fuck the grass for making me love it and the sea and hot tea and window
  steam and felt tip pens and afghans with granny squares and the
  word *belly*.
Fuck this painful, sweet, fleeting, beautiful shit. Fuck all of it.

Places on the Body

1.

Two artists, my mother and I talk about a tunnel
that appears to breathe, a place to enter, made of oiled

paper, lit and red. We imagine a chicken-wire room,
round, hair woven through the crosspieces,

and the way one might curl there, marsupial.
We talk about a wound made of cheesecloth

and pinked newsprint, something sinister—a shard
of hambone—poking through. She knits a tube,

a fissure, an os, and I make an egg of blue
tissue to go inside so the string stretches,

strained. She tells me a secret: she believes
a painting made of innards would be beautiful.

2.

She can't say what it all means—there's a hole
in everything she paints, surfaces sanded away,

canvases layered over weeks, burned, greased,
gouged, until they become places both tender

and ferocious, until to look at one of them
is to feel afraid and ashamed and exhilarated.

They make me hurt, like watching a man
get his knees broken in a gangster film,

watching a goat give birth, like a gill
or fontanel, that delicate pulse below the skin.

3.

What if someone grows inside you,
a clot, a frog, a baby bear,

what if you become, while this bear
becomes, some place tender and ferocious,

some place round and warm and red,
and when this bear breaks out, leaving you

a little broken, your edges raw, in need
of stitching up, your body makes food,

you spend a year or two or three with this bear's
pursed mouth and pink bum and shiny feet

curled around you in the bed, the car,
the restaurant bathroom, its eyes an unreal

blue and always on you because
you're delicious, you can tell by the way

this bear growls and kneads and its blue
bear eyes roll hour after hour.

4.

Until he eats bread. Rice. Banana. Like the small hole
a bullet makes in metal, its ragged edges curved.

Lunchbox. Like the roof blown off, cone of wind
scooping indiscriminately. School bus, oh sweet god,

a hole in the ground so the dead and living
mingle, the bones of dinosaurs, the moon shining

from the other side of the earth. Dirty chat rooms
and prescription drugs. A lie. Another lie. Something

as ordinary as a car crash or a perfectly lovely girl
the bear would like to marry. A painting made

of innards, harrowing and beautiful. Wound
so big it's edgeless. Boundless opening, sublime.

Elegy for Fireflies

Each month, we climbed four flights of stairs,
wanting to see you written in light

against a screen's bruised gray,
but time after time the midwife

didn't offer sonogram, only let us listen.
She pressed the gadget against my belly

and we heard the muffled feedback
of your movements, arms and legs thrashing

in a distant bath, and then the noise of a heart
the size of a grape seed—galloping.

Sometimes on the stairs we'd encounter
another patient leaning on the banister,

hiding her face or crying without shame,
a terrible, wretched wail. What could we say

to this woman descending
so different now from us?

In the sixth month, the stairs were clear,
quiet, and we hurried to the little room

where we'd get our dose of you, be assured
we had indeed made a baby, weren't like those kids

from grade school always claiming white ponies
and trampolines no one ever saw.

This time, though, the Doppler reported
only static, steady scratch and hiss—

no sign of you. The midwife strolled off
to fetch the ultrasound, and while we waited,

holding hands, we heard from the next room
wailing, that familiar wet howl,

a woman seeing stillness, her baby
unmoving on the monitor.

In that moment, we were childless too,
you just a story we'd told on the playground.

We'd have to give up our fond wish,
the hope that if we said a thing enough

it could be true. When the midwife came back
wheeling the machine, we felt sure she'd find

nothing, but you appeared, bug in a jar.
There you were, buzzing with blood. There you were,

but what had been born already was your loss,
and we'd go nowhere without it anymore.

Waiting Song with Dioramas
9 months pregnant

My husband hates a predator, can't abide
fang or claw. But at the museum, I adore
the frozen scenes behind glass, time
stopped at last, so my own slowed brain

can take what it wants—the polished eye,
the plaster teeth, almost-clash of beast
and lesser beast. I need the unnatural
stillness, nascent space in which nothing

transpires yet—each moment a dusty frond
that, always and never delicate, cannot
unfurl. But also, waiting, I wish
to resign myself to *nature*. At each tableau

I say like a mantra, *These things happen*,
till my man, himself a tender shoot,
his hand softly at the small of my back,
presses me toward the next window.

My body, swollen with cargo I'll carry
forward, then let go whether I wish it
or not, is happy to linger here, too—
where early humans squat

by a meager fire, shearing meat
from bones, a woman nursing blankly,
nipples that droop to her lap. Or here
where a couple, heavy browed

and lightly furred but otherwise built
like us, regards a terrifying bird
just wingbeats from their necks.
My husband, himself expecting,

himself a clenched fist, prepares
to hurl his body between even this
still threat and any hunted thing—rabbit,
seal, waxy baby swaddled in its sleep.

Early Labor with Ice Storm

This morning, cracking
woke me. At the window, trees

broken, white sapwood
startled as the inside of bones.

III.

Already the world, the world.

And you are slipping
down, away from my heart.

victoria redel

Postnatal Epithalamium

She'd be another wedding we always said, coil of genes,
you and me truly twined for good. But here's the thing:
this marriage eats, it cries, it rarely ever sleeps.

I can cheat on you in my dreams, but *she* won't let me
have dreams. I'm like the waking dead in those movies,
mad at the still-alive and the all-the-way-gone—at least

they can rest. None of this walking around moaning,
dripping from the breast. It isn't that we want to divorce.
Yes, there's the squabbling, but bitterness is tempered

by the blush of love, afternoons agape at her fractal
beauty, ear and fist and the swirl of red at her crown.
I learn to say aloud what I want to believe, four a.m.

pacing, her sad piglet sounds, me cooing *You
are the gift I wished for, every day like Christmas.*
And it's true—she's a jewel I produced in the shape

of my heart or liver or spleen, something bloodthirsty
and essential. I just need a nap. Eventually it comes,
sweet lozenge, fully dissolved in three hours time,

but I'm not greedy. I start to wake with a smile
on my face, ready to unwrap the baby and myself,
ready to sop up gratitude like a rich breakfast. Still,

you and I give up on the idea of intimacy by DNA,
most of our kisses made of air and the waving of hands.
By now I've chosen between you and the baby more times

than I care to remember. There's a tingling in the breast
and she wins out, a tingling lower down, it's you. Remember
how we used to say we'd *live together*? I'm learning why

we need ceremony, words to remind us how to get through
what we once thought would be easy. Married as I am
to her hunger, I can still say this to you: I do.

I Watch *Nature* While Breastfeeding

The bat threads night with ribbons
of sound, and everywhere her call gets lost
she flies. Sometimes the sky
reveals itself a trail of crumbs, sometimes
a maze of walls, trees. Before her,
flight, food, fracture, and only her voice
tells which is which—self and stone,
self and moth, self and nothing.

Behind a fan of sticks and straw
like the wave of a hand, shy and slow,
a bowerbird makes a pretty cave, open
at beak and tail, tunnel he lines with twine
and slivers of bone. While he sleeps, he dreams
of the beloved, her tufted head, her sheen,
and another bird tramples, takes
a red button, pink shell.

I accept the delicate inhalation of skin
at your skull, pulse too thin to hear.
From the door in to the door out—sometimes
only a bird's length. Still, I'll take what our bodies
offer, unfold my own appetites and tell you
all the world hungers. See how the bats,
singing their blind song, swoop
the night to fill their tiny bellies?

Labor Aubade

Here is the cold I've crawled into,
out of the damp warren of the bed
where you and our little daughter lie.

Lately she'll drink milk from a cup;
I'm going out to write. I'm giving
up your skin's warmth, breath-music,

hands and feet reaching each other's
bodies, all that accidental connection
before you take the day's polite

positions. I've promised to return
bearing gifts, story of how light wakes
slow and blue, of how the dark's

dissolving belly holds morning
with its long shadow, its surge
of traffic and coffee smell.

At nine, after three hours of solitude
and aching breasts, I'll call home,
where there will have been only

absolutes, black and then brilliance
striping into our rooms, silence
then the metallic exhalation

of a school bus at the curb.
Aware I have traded each detail
of your waking in order to wake

to myself, this other self, again,
I'll release at least a small sun
from where it swelled a whole

sleepless night. I'll write. I'll write.
Others will, hours from now, line up
at the glass and visit what's born, already

bathed and dressed, but I'll see it break out,
blood-polished, and in its first burning
eclipse everything I could lose.

Bruise

for Annabelle, walking

It's almost beautiful
what the skin can do:

bloom. A stain
like a violet opening

its blue on the silk
of your cheek. Once

an organ of mine, born
you're a lost lung

and I'm half breathless.
You've fallen from some height

and your journey
marked you. I can't ignore

what has risen
to the surface: tenderness,

your body's reminder
there's only

the skin's distance
between here and gone.

Echolocation

Five dry days after your purple arrival
you sucked and cried, till suddenly benevolence

let down. Then a frenzy of communion,
no way to doubt the bread became

your body, paper skin pinked, fine bones
hidden beneath milk transmogrified.

I stayed naked, cut the split second of button
through hole so you never had to cry,

wails of neighbor kids through the walls
untranslatable and faint, even your father

a stranger on a bus, banished
from the kingdom of touch, the breasts he'd held,

one in each palm, their silk and heft a balm
for dreams of falling. Now you're two years old.

They say when a child begins to ask
the time has come to refuse

so who wouldn't vow silence given the choice?
This morning, unlatching with room in your belly

for the toast your father stood buttering,
you said, *This nipple looks like a flower.*

But come midnight, here you are
making small ranging sounds, *mama*

and *more*, and I think of bats, their wrinkled noses
and skin-wings, their hunger sonic.

Each cry gauges the space between
what they hope for and their mouths.

Epithalamium with Trigger Warning

Because some raw deal or double
allele makes me afraid for myself

and on behalf of every single
person in the world, each stranger

seems to be my shooter and my child.
So I watch you, stranger, in the café,

the library, the theater's red plush
lobby: the way you hide one hand

in jacket pocket, the way you
clutch your camo backpack

or your seam-ripped lovey duck
and suck your thumb.

Your real mother's gaze astray,
I shadow you today, trailing

from counter to corner, ticket booth
to mezzanine. Like a cop eyeing

eyes and brow, bruises and frown,
I guess your tremulous intentions.

My chest aches. I lose
my breath. I

love you. I
love you.

Damage

She says it when she stubs her toe,
when there's no more mango,

when the cup stack tumbles,
with a door slam, wolfish,

when I send her to her room.
She's misheard *damn it*, lucky

accident, but also this mistake
isn't one, *damage* the right word

for what the world does,
throbbing us with hunger

or defeat. Even love is damage
or its aftermath. I think of the word

prune, as in the necessary cutting
back, stack of limber limbs snipped

perhaps in their prime, in order
to ensure a bigger tree. That gloved

hand that holds the shears? That's
me, and both of us bleed.

Stabat Mater Dolorosa

The daughter, roundly praised by experts
in the field of folly, starts to swell.
By the time we near the building

she's outgrown me, my umbrella nothing
but a smart cap atop her distant head.
Apostrophes, they said, *like no other child.*

And that smile. I'm drenched and trailing,
an ornament, a poodle, a fob. Still,
she's my job. We're hours greasing the door

and a crowd forms. With a raised hand
she keeps them dry and blinks away
their compliments like flies.

She is now quite literally above the fray.
I say she's difficult in private, won't eat
frozen peas, corrects her grandmother's speech.

With her thumbnail she carves the letter A
into everything. *A gourmand!*
A grammarian! A scribe! There is no

subtling them. They adulate endlessly
the way obsessed French lovers blow
kisses on TV. It occurs to me

she may only be full of hot air
and I stop struggling to shove her in
and begin to search for the sort of valve

through which you blew your breath
into those plastic jobs from the county fair—
Bugs Bunny, Betty Boop, and once a wrestler

three feet high who, weighted by a bladder
of black sand, wobbled when you punched him
in the head. But no—she's as seamless

as a cloud, even her own mug smugged
shut by now. I worry she'll burst
and as the crowd begins to climb the ribs

of her big socks, as they reach her dress hem,
I panic. I poke her with a pen nib
which peppers her with a circle of tiny holes

like the speaker of an old-timey radio
and the tinny voice says *don't*. I can't stop
stabbing, though, and it's for her own good—

the French lovers climb and clamor
and her skin grows tight.
That's when I decide to bite.

For a moment she flies, shedding
little citizens and shooting skyward
till she's nothing but a scrap,

some kid's red kite unmoored, a cardinal.
But all too soon she takes another shape.
Looping back toward us, she's a dress,

a shoe, an empty head, and now instead
of the daughter (once so robust, full of
punctuation and promise), a spent balloon,

a wrinkled hide with spit inside, settles
at my feet. Though I always do the best I can
with breast and hand, with peanut butter

and unit blocks, with timeout and fairy tale,
with pen and teeth, I fail. So I say
to those still gathered, fingers pointed

and mouths agape, *Just wait*.
And I *will* try, to smooth the hide,
seal the rent that vented hers

and blow my sad air in. But here's the thing:
since mother means to mistake,
I have known for many years it is too late.

Love Song with Vehophobia

That dream of skulls like eggshells, their terrible
marrow, the vein in your wrist, daughter, the vein

in your neck, collision of bird and glass and the idea
of your organs, like birds—(some of us are alive now,

and some of us are dead)—my uncle's pelvis
puzzled pieces, his chest a sunken steering wheel.

Open rear window: a cousin flying, flown.
I saw him later on a stretcher, like a cat under

blankets, the black bag at his mouth my mother said
would *help*. I remember the day we brought you home,

your father steady at the wheel, but the sun looked
crazy and the other cars full of strangers who couldn't

know how long I'd waited, how your birth split me.
I sat next to your car seat, one hand on your

robin's egg head, the other moving over you, not sure
which part to protect. And anyway, apart from

home, where is there to go that's worth the risk?
Not fishing, not shopping, certainly not—*Jesus Christ*—

the airport. My cousin is dead, a little ghost at the foot
of his father's bed, that wheel still pressed into

my uncle's chest, and something presses my chest, too.
The day is bright, daughter, the house okay. *Let's stay.*

How to Pray without Ceasing

Pricked on the word *lance*, I
try to soothe on *whisper, minaret,*

suck *wristlet* like a strand
of hair, sniff the air for *violet.*

The phrase *a Friday night*
stabs too because there are only

so many, so tender I am on
spine, on *fingertip,* on *skinless* and *kiss.*

Now hear this: *winter moon*
and *shooter. Spinal tap* and

endless bliss of *filibuster, cabaret,*
helicopter, coronet, and underneath

a *concertina*, tiny music only I
can hear, oh, *halcyon*, the perfect

past, mythical mother who lays
her egg on dangerous waters and decides,

because of *delicate*, because of *hunger*
pang, not to fly away.

IV.

Every day now I feel myself
pressed harder into this life.

Sometimes it's so near and docile
I can feel my hand take hold of it.

Other times it's that old, alarming
grief, that animal scrambling

to its feet, desperate
to be living.

carrie fountain

Apologia with Generalized Anxiety Disorder

1.

Maybe my soft parts hardening, maybe nodes
grown, certainly teeth ground to crumbs
in my mouth? Eventually. Or if not mine,

someone's, and I spend nights, covert,
feeling for strange organs through
my husband's skin. The shape I'm in.

I need a hymnal, something to sing when ghosts
crowd the foot of our bed. I need a word
to stop the wheeling in my head. It might be

never. It might be now. Something tells me
I'm swollen. Maybe objects in the distance blur?
I train my eye on the window, imagining

a terrible blindness, till a bat squeezes in
through a hole the size of a quarter and then
sudden frantic flight. Now he clutches a curtain

and quiets. The house snores on, and I'm torn
between wanting to crush him, *oh possible
pestilence*, and wanting him to stay, safe—

his tiny furred body, tender snout.
But I catch him between tennis rackets
and outside gentle him against a tree

till his claws clutch bark. Now he clicks
into vast black, listening his way home.
If his body's poison waits to craze him,

he doesn't know it. In bed again, eyes closed,
I count the many awful things I know and all
that floats unnamable behind my lids.

2.

In this one I marry Charles Ingalls and he burns in a locked barn
In this one all my teeth click into the sink
In this one bandits shoot my father
bandits shoot me
In this one you have decided not to love me
or you have decided you never loved me
In this one you love me but I can't find you
your phone number a puzzle
In this one you don't know me
When I pound on your door you send your brother
to muscle me away
In this one we crouch in a basement
bombs whistle and I wish I had looked at your face more often
I wish I had not been afraid to say—
In this one the tip of a tree sprouts from our dog's belly
and when we pull, she slides to the floor, empty
In this one our dog escapes into mad streets
and when I follow, I find the town full of dogs almost her
In this one I have a baby that turns into a cat
I have a baby and put it in boiling water
In this one I have a baby and put it in the freezer
I have a baby and I don't know where she is
or I know where she is but my mother keeps her from me
In this one my mother says she hates me
In this one I have no mother
When I wake, I still have no mother
How can I have written such a thing?

3.

For this I'm sorry: I was a baby born
clenched at the center, and some infection,

some poisoned marrow
made my bones ache till my mother

couldn't take my cries.
Now, like a spy I watch myself, waiting

for that bad news, recurring,
to rise to the surface, redden my skin

and radiate a pain about which
it is impossible to remain silent.

Skydiver

(for my little sister, coming out)

Afternoons you cartwheeled, six years old
and clumsy, across our unmowed lawn
in your grass-stained sweat suit, your left eye

lazy, right eye sticker-patched beneath
thick glasses and crooked, mom-cut bangs.
From kitchen window I watched you

concentrate and flail, fall
and rise and cartwheel, some days until
the sky got dark or the knees of your pants

bled through. *Dogged* you were, are,
in your pursuit of what your body *might not*
do. These days I see you, some stranger

strapped to your back, leaping from plane
into terror, screaming glory into that thin air.
I see the scars that braid above your wrist's

metal plate, your spine's wrong turn,
your fist fights with schizophrenic veterans
on the ward where you nurse nights.

I see you in plaid and winged eyeliner
in the Dyke March. Little sister,
you press your tender chest into

the frightening, falling world as though
to get up in this fucker's face might be
the only way to suffer its slings,

65

its sweet and sorry flings, its kisses
and cuts, as though you meant
to cartwheel into fist after fist forever.

Forgiftet Garden

That long, ugly winter over, I still can't
put aside the death of the young giraffe
at Copenhagen, shot by keepers
while he lipped chunks of rye bread

in the zoo. And I'm sad because, brother,
you're always lying—today you call to say
you're mad with pain from kidney stones
the size of walnuts and since you can't have

painkillers, you've asked the doctor again
for the methadone our father has begged
she not prescribe. I cry for the stones,
which don't exist and which you say

may take months to pass, and for your
mutilating need, which does and will never.
I can't walk the prettiest road
in our neighborhood this spring—the one

with flowering trees that rain pink
blossoms that brown almost before
they hit the ground and fill the air
with a scent like dying jasmine

and star fruit—because a rabbit lies
melting into a tuft of grass in front
of one house unrented since March.
Did you know after they culled

that healthy calf, wrong
for the breeding scheme, they fed
his body to lions while a crowd watched
from behind a fence? I can't look too long

at little boys at the grocery store, the park,
with freckled cheeks like yours and curly
hair so thick and cut so short it looks like fur.
Did you know the Danish word for poison

is *gift*? You tried heroin at fourteen.
What did you want? You nuzzled from some
sweet hand while another you couldn't detect
reached around to seize your slender neck.

Still Life with Geese and Oxycontin

Brother, we heard your hunger cries; we rose
to bring your milk. Now you eat pills
and sleep with skinny women, blue ghosts

of other men's names inked on their breastbones.
We kindled to sounds of your keening will.
Brother, we heard your hunger cries and rose.

Dad told me years ago the bird let loose
from the back of that deep V is feeble,
that he'll wing toward a flock of ghosts

till sister, mother, father from him go
and, like breath, his own unsung will
evaporates. Brother, you cried. We rose,

and rise, at least as far as wishing goes
(although you strut and stagger, steal
and stick around). So like our own, your ghosts,

your hollow honking song. We can't let go.
Neither can we stay, hover still,
abide your hungry cries. And if instead we rose
to ours, what then of you, oh brother, ghost?

Love Song with Helplessness

Somewhere dirt and blood
make dark mud as ground
explodes. Somewhere a stranger

waits to shell my brother into bits,
and I keep crawling inside words.
Today I'm with *bowl* and *balm*,

their sound soothing the air,
their sense a hidey hole,
the hush between two hands.

I'm hoping these cupped palms
make a *tourniquet*, that this calm
extends to him, an *epithem*.

The War, the War, Christmas

My brother, given short reprieve
in the form of six blackened
tumors stacked like coals along

his spine, will languish stateside
till the new year. Then he'll learn
to shoot the cannon he will aim

at strangers who will aim their guns
at him, his pink scar and the same
blue eyes he wore when he was born.

I sit in the bathtub and cry—
relief, dread, helplessness. Unless
the mess at his back turns uglier,

by spring he'll be in Afghanistan,
and even if, by grace, he lives,
there is no chance he will not kill.

I zipped him into jammies.
Once when he had a sore toe,
I filled a bowl with Epsom salts,

a rubber duck afloat above
his tiny feet. I gave him books
and modeling clay and rubber stamps.

Sometimes, scared in the darkest
part of night, he dragged
his sleeping bag to my room

and lay on the floor near my bed.
I'd find him in the morning,
those mouth-open snores.

Grown and gone when he
was not yet three, I dreamed
my parents left open the door

to the basement, night after night,
that baby falling down the stairs.
Now, awake, I think that dream

is true—not him exploded
on some desert road, but gone—
that baby, that boy,

without a lick of violence—
disappeared. You don't know this
when you're young: how time

kills children, every one of them
you ever loved, and nothing
you can do. My own girl, too—

once so fat at the cheek, curved
against my chest all through the night—
Annabelle has breasts, tiny, like stones

beneath the skin, like omens,
and whenever I kiss this little girl,
I'm kissing her goodbye.

This is the way I lose one baby
every day. The war, the war,
Saturday. Christmas. Goodbye.

Nom de Guerre
for Annabelle

She wants to know what we'd have called her
had she been born a boy. I'd still have called her
purple stranger, emergent property. Cries-

for-milk. Would still have wanted to lick
her clean. *Eliot* is what she means, the name
we picked for our possible son, the one

who occupied me along with her until
the box opened. She asks if it's *gender neutral*.
When I hatched *Eliot* from sleep, woke with it

on my lips, I saw the small brown-haired boy
from the movie, child who could love even
the least recognizable friend without reserve,

who felt the alien's longing like a wheeze
in his own chest—*ouch*. She doesn't want to *be*
Eliot, I tell myself, just wants to imagine

how it feels to be born in a body she can dress
in suits and ties, feel buttoned and battened,
and create no antecedent error, no phantom

ache. She wants different words, a different
world. What would we call that place? In that place,
what would we call this child? Home?

One Reason to Stay

Yes—I'm still hungry. Last night
in a dream I ate fists of flour, dry white

caking my mouth till I couldn't
breathe, but listen: whoever tells you

sixteen is the time of your life
is wrong.

Sixteen was a bathtub of busted tile,
can of pig meat from catholic charity,

mother—dying,
father—fishing,

boy after sweaty boy with his fingers
at the buckle of my jeans.

Sixteen was mean.
I tried to sleep through it

but the alarm kept going off.
Now there are nights I can't sleep at all

for the worry—bills, breast lumps,
cracks in the cellar walls—

but it's two dozen years since
I locked the bedroom door

and pen-knifed my forearms,
the thin skin of my thighs,

since I traced the blue wrist line
I might cut if one more fool told me

it doesn't get any better. It did,
in a million ways I can't say

because the language of forty
and sixteen have so few words

in common. I can tell you this: last night
I woke choking to find a warm man

willing to scoop the ghost flour
from my mouth with a kiss.

Meanwhile

What are we all, but bits of time caught for a moment
in a tangle of blood, bones, skin, and brain?
LOUISE ERDRICH

In the gypsy language, the word for tomorrow
is the same as the word for today, everything

that's coming—here. It's always Christmas,
we're already dust, so I collapse the myth

of progress—light from dead stars, the evolution
of bones. Our wanting and our moans such

cousins, such kissing clones, I long and am lit
at once, the way a house is all electric, wrapped

and threaded with a constant charge. I read
there are birds who fly in their sleep, and asleep

I dream I can fly. Once the phrase *a Friday night*
wracked me with cries—there are only so many

and we don't know when we're having the last,
but now, my gypsy, all Fridays converge, on my lips

every margarita I'll ever sip, and the salt of your skin
loosening, like the miracle of lost and found

and lost. What am I but a girl moving in a coffin
of glass or falling from a fabulous mezzanine?

Who are you but a baby, a prince, a dead man
with your arms open, flakes of ash on a wind?

For you I'd undo the moon—already a splinter—
all of us off course, undone. My singleton, my

footsore scavenger, your pockets full of flowers
and stones, your days—dawn-dark, full of promise

and the promise of sleep. The promise of waking
in a future already flying, already, already flown.

Dear Terror, Dear Splendor

Yes, I realize wishing all the horrors
that will ever befall me or that I'll ever
witness or hear about or even imagine

were over already
might be the same
as wishing to be dead.

But what can I say?
Dear Terror, Dear Splendor, Annabelle
got her learner's permit today.

Remember when that chicken, pecking for feed, bit her finger
and I spent months fearing tetanus? Remember when a bat
bloomed into the house through a hole in the window screen

and my brain throbbed *rabies* for a year or when she cut
her foot, hit her head, coughed
black blood, was born

with a fever
a softspot
a self?

Dear Terror, driving home on date night
we came upon a group of teenagers
who, bound for the prom, had struck a deer

and stood in the street bewildered
by its body so other drivers swerved
around their sobbing, sequined

congress, which caused one car
to summersault and I saw an arm cut
loose from its window and still do.

But often I am made love to so sweetly,
Dear Splendor, so expertly that the world
ceases to exist or simply

doesn't matter, birth and death
and blood and breath
compressed, this body, this bed.

Dear Splendor, Dear Terror, we doubled
our danger this way or grew it by a factor
I don't know how, don't want, to name.

Nights I still step into the slatted moon glow
of our child's bedroom—our *child*, seventeen,
stretched aslant, asleep, across her double bed,

banking hours against the forever
she'll soon start spending
                                    not here—

and if I can't see in that near-dark her torso
rise and fall, I lean in and listen for her breath.
I've heard it every time so far.

Perpetual Beginner

Outside, everything starts to rot till
the world is wine, that dark and sour
and a little sweet despite its dying.
In here, my hair fades, a frown line
deepening, and I can't ignore anymore
that no one has called me young lady
this year. Still, I keep feeling like
the same girl, all the while more
womanish, more in love with myself.
What kind of wealth grows as you
spend it? I don't know, but I'm getting
richer in this body, achy knees,
and it's harder to see, and my belly
hangs a little when you're behind me
in our bed, another happy birthday.
Afterward, there's a chill in the air,
the window still open—we can hear
the neighbors fight, nothing serious,
one dog barking and then another,
and we pull up the covers, July's
sick heat a bad dream we're
forgetting. Some days, I take it
personally, the way the years have
amounted to this. Tonight
I just fall asleep in your arms, and—
like magic—I'm somebody's baby again.

V.

I want to tell you what happened
when I let her go, but I don't understand it yet.

kerrin mccadden

Some Say the World

for Annabelle, on her 18th birthday

1.

I started an uneasy tally years ago
while you, still tiny, ate your first muffin,
oven warm. From your fingers butter dripped
down your dimpled arms, CNN silent
behind you, towers collapsing

and collapsing.
I kept the tally, too, while I rocked you
in a cozy darkness lit by sudden, shocking
bursts of fire and smoke rising from Kabul
as it fell. What kind of world
could I give you, give you to?

For *birth*,
Spanish speakers say *dar luz*, to give light.
Now we hold candles in Lafayette Square Park,
twelve thousand vigilant
in the President's backyard, and I weep
so loudly strangers console me, offering
their arms across the flickering dark.

*My mother feels things
deeply*, you explain to the tall woman
in the pussy hat, the dapper man in plaid
who told us bigots call a child born
to undocumented parents on U.S. soil
an *anchor baby*.

Darling girl,
this is not the hour in which I hoped
you'd come of age.

2.

At four you kept a beetle—a lifeless
Fiery Searcher—vivid green and copper
carapace unmoving on a bed of cotton
in a little box beneath my reading lamp,
and day after day I let you believe
that meager heat might resurrect it.
How awful and how sweet to wake
to your face, hopeful, at my nightstand.

Am I a coward? It's my job to be to you
the bearer of good news
and bad—nest of hatchlings,
                    sun-bleached bone—
and I've tried to deserve it, spent
hours, years, abiding
as you dropped stick after stick
into the brook from one side of a bridge,
then crossed with you to wait for each one
to come into view on the other side.

Now what will come
                    into view, my daughter,
I'm afraid to know, but *you*—
I don't have to tell you that beetle's dead.
You're a citizen of *this*
future. Your near-grown face is beautiful,
is brave. You believe in science
and revolt. You tell me some flowers
won't open
            till they burn.

3.

Today I watch video of an Iraq War vet
shooting strangers in a Florida airport
then spend the next hour trying to soothe myself
with a clip that shows a man freeing a sparrow
frozen to a metal fence post by holding
the little body in his big hand and breathing
on its feet until the ice melts.

    That November night when you returned
    home after sixteen hours feeding ballots
    into the box in an elementary school gym
    on a county road that winds between
    scrub pines and shacks,
                 you knew,
    but I gripped your father's hand
    before the TV and told you, *No—*
    It's too soon to call!
               You went to bed.
    In the morning, I steadied myself to offer
    the comfort I thought you'd need
    from me. Instead you declared,
                    This
    is what happens before the revolution.

Onscreen the man breathes
on those delicate feet again, the bird
afraid until the moment
he opens his gloved hand.

I can't tell whether I breathe or you do.
Or I can, and it shames me. Or I can,
      and it thrills me. *Go ahead and fly,*
the man says.
           Go ahead and fly—

NOTES

Section I's epigraph is from Rita Dove's "Lamentations."

Section II's epigraph is from Theodore Roethke's "What Can I Tell My Bones?"

Section III's epigraph is from Victoria Redel's "Ninth Month."

Section IV's epigraph is from Carrie Fountain's "Burn Lake 2."

Section V's epigraph is from Kerrin McCadden's "Passerines."

Cirque du Crève-Cœur can be translated as "Circus of Heartbreak."

The epigraph for "Grounded" comes from Robert Frost's "Birches."

The opening line of "Epithalamium with Acrobats" takes inspiration from a line in Matthew Arnold's "Dover Beach."

Stabat Mater Dolorosa can be translated as "stands the mother, full of grief."

Forgiftet can be translated as both "poisoned" and "forgiven."

The epigraph for "Meanwhile" comes from Louise Erdrich's *Four Souls*.

The title of "Perpetual Beginner" comes from Theodore Roethke's "What Can I Tell My Bones?"

ACKNOWLEDGMENTS

I would like to thank the editors of the following journals in which these poems, sometimes with different titles and in slightly different versions, first appeared:

The Asheville Poetry Review: "Meanwhile"
The Atlanta Review: "Old Man and Nurse" and "Instead of Prayer"
The Boiler: "*Forgiftet* Garden" and "Still Life with Geese and Oxycontin"
The Café Review: "Epithalamium with Acrobats"
Calyx: A Journal of Art and Literature by Women: "I Watch Nature While Breastfeeding"
Connotation Press: An Online Artifact: "One Reason to Stay," "Skydiver," and "Waiting Song with Dioramas"
The Cortland Review: "Southbound Epithalamium"
Crab Orchard Review: "Bruise" and "Labor Aubade"
The Florida Review: "Nom de Guerre"
From East to West: Bicoastal Verse: "Love Song to a Cashier," "Perpetual Beginner," and "Postnatal Epithalamium"
Glass: A Journal of Poetry: "Some Say the World"
Lifeboat: A Journal of Memoir: "Elegy for Fireflies"
Literary Mama: "Damage"
Lumina: "Love Song with Vehophobia"
Nelle: "Mourning Portrait for Uncle Steve" and "A Laying On of Hands"
Seneca Review: "*Stabat Mater Dolorosa*"
The Shallow Ends: "Dear Terror, Dear Splendor"
Words and Images: "This River"

"This River" won the Betsy Sholl Award for Poetry from the University of Southern Maine in 2011.

dancing girl press published some of these poems in a chapbook entitled *Cirque du Crève-Cœur* in 2008.

Finishing Line Press published some of these poems in a chapbook entitled *Girl, Giant* in 2013.

I am grateful to the Barbara Deming/Money for Women Fund for generous support of my work.

I am grateful, too, to the friends who first read these poems and loved them and me enough to help make them better. Bottomless thanks to my Portland, Maine, workshop group (Michael Macklin, Peter Manuel, Marita O'Neill, Betsy Sholl, Bruce Spang, Kathleen Sullivan, Jim Thatcher, and Cathryn Wilson) and my Asheville, North Carolina, workshop group in all its incarnations (Nickole Brown, Briar DeHaven, Luke Hankins, Jessica Jacobs, Matthew Olzmann, Rachel Shopper, Brian Sneeden, Nomi Stone, and Lucy Tobin). Thanks, too, to Rachel Contreni Flynn for lending her sharp eye to an earlier version of this manuscript that isn't the final version precisely because of her insight. And special thanks to Jessica Jacobs for her wisdom and generosity, her magic-level capacity to help me figure out what this book wanted and needed, and for critiques so clear and so kind and so good they sometimes make me cry.

There's no way outside these poems to adequately express my gratitude to the people and places that made me and from which I made these poems. To my kin (by blood, by shared space both inner and outer) and to the landscape of Aroostook County, Maine, I say forgive me, and you're welcome, and thank you, thank you, thank you. May we keep finding ourselves in each other.

Annabelle, you blessed and transformed me by being born to me, and I have honed my voice to your ear ever since.

Oh, Mark—*I hope you know. I hope you know.* What you haven't given me (helped me find, bear, celebrate, or make), I don't have.

WISCONSIN POETRY SERIES

Edited by Ronald Wallace

(B) = WINNER OF THE BRITTINGHAM PRIZE IN POETRY
(FP) = WINNER OF THE FELIX POLLAK PRIZE IN POETRY
(4L) = WINNER OF THE FOUR LAKES PRIZE IN POETRY